The Kids Who Live On The Moon

Jim Carter

A collection of poems by the Tramping Artisan

labyrinthe

LABYRINTHE PRESS | www.labyrinthepress.com

Jim Carter/Labyrinthe Press
Leigh-on-Sea, United Kingdom
www.labyrinthepress.com

Book Layout © 2015 BookDesignTemplates.com
Printed by CreateSpace, Charleston SC
Available from Amazon.com and other retail outlets

British Library Cataloguing in Publication Data
The Kids Who Live On The Moon/ Jim Carter. -- 1st ed.
ISBN 978-0-9932029-2-6 (print edition)
ISBN 978-0-9932029-3-3 (electronic edition)

This book is dedicated in love to
The graceful memory of Avril,
The strength and beauty of Amy,
The gentle presence of Bobbie.

Contents

Foreword

What's the purpose of a new book of poems? As a reader, this question must accompany any purchase of a work of this kind, even for an ardent fan of poetry.

For me, one important object is to stir the soul – to inspire and provoke, to delight and, at times, to disturb. Poems that speak directly from one heart to another are the ones that most capture my attention.

This collection achieves this intention with admirable ease. Jim Carter is a poet who wears his heart on his sleeve, exposes his wounds and doesn't shy away from keeping the passion at the core of his being from shining through. He skilfully knits words and metaphors, creating lively pictures of the very human scenes that he describes.

Sometimes mundane, down-to-earth and unsophisticated; at other times, expounding philosophical thought and parody, he jumps between different rhyme schemes, between humour and profound sadness, and between the contemporary and the past.

His subject matter is as varied as his styles. Scenes of childhood, young romance and parting all feature, but so too do a mix of delightful vignettes that are bound to bring a smile to anyone's face, possibly also mixed with moments of happy reminiscing.

I first met Jim whilst we were both students at interfaith seminary. This followed an incredibly sad period for him, which he managed with grace and magnanimity. We formed an immediate bond. Jim's brilliant humour, humility and forthrightness appealed to my love of honesty and disregard for pretension. Jim would always speak in plain terms, being ready to go alone if need be to stand up for something he believed in. He is deeply compassionate – practical and sincere in his giving to others, a real friend who can be depended upon.

It therefore came as no surprise to me that these poems reflect Jim's humanity. With his sharp insight and a clear gift for crafting the written word, they are a joy to absorb time and again.

I became familiar with Jim's poems somewhat late into our training together. By this time, I'd come to know him as a travelling minstrel, as accomplished in writing and performing soul-stirring songs as he is a writer of poetry.

Of course, many of his songs are poems that have been set to music. Here, they are allowed to speak for themselves. They inspire wonder, provoking a depth of feeling, and bringing delight. These are the stories that often did come true for kids who live on the moon.

Clive Johnson
Poet and author

Introduction

It's an early August afternoon in 2015. I'm sat in a cafe at the Festival Hall in London. The view overlooks the Thames and the place is loud with the buzz of tourists, day-trippers and office workers taking a break before getting back on the wheel. A few of us occupy tables on our own; only one of the four seats taken. They, like me, are either typing into an electronic device or are buried deep in the pages of a book.

Today I feel is not a day to write poetry. But then again, I saw the children on the South Bank screaming with delight as they dodged in and out of the water fountains, dressed in holiday swimming costumes and conveying that innocent school holiday joy that we all remember so vividly. Maybe this is the poem today? But no, I just don't feel it; that feeling that usually starts with a play on words that sum up an entire page. That sits with me sometimes for days, and then one day an ejaculation of words and phrases just pours out. I sit back and look at what is there on the page and I know almost immediately whether this will survive the black biro strike out. The rule as always is, "if it moves me then it lives".

More recently I have been playing with poetic structure. I've been building sonnets, villanelles, triolets and learning to Ghazal. I see how I am slowly being pulled further and further into that place, that world we call poetry. I once said, to a friend of mine, "I'm a poet". He said "don't be ridiculous". I asked him why he thought this. He explained that, if that was the case and I was a poet, then he might as well call himself one too. "But you don't write poetry" I said. "If you did then you would be a poet". This was important to me as I hear so many times people saying what they want to be, when in fact they are. "I want to be a photographer," "I want to be a painter," and so on. Yet she has been taking photographs for years and his bedroom is full of completed canvasses. So I declare what I am and I allow you to decide if the words move you.

While I find writing poems to be extremely therapeutic and spiritual, the hard part is always in introducing them to an audience, putting them on the air. So, in my mediations on this I came up with a wonderful solution – "Just get them out there." This is where the idea for this book came into being. By the time I had written a body of poems I had already been writing them for a few years, although the last two years have seen a bow wave of verse appear. Also, in my song writing I am increasingly putting poems to music. Then my dear friend, fellow interfaith minister, writer and publisher Clive Johnson, agreed to publish my poems. So what about this collection? Well I don't want to say too much about the poems in one respect. As I unravel the stories of some of these pieces then it may deny the reader the agency for some of the words to resonate with them in a way that I wouldn't have envisaged. In this way a poem can tell several tales and touch different hearts for different reasons.

The poems I write are written from how I experience the world. In that sense I suppose they are deeply personal. I have in the past tried to write about things outside of my experience and it always comes out as facile or feels like mock profundity. This is when we devalue words by seeing them as just a set of syllabic patterns that make a hierarchy of impact depending on how obscure the word or how unbelievably flowery the word. The irony then for me is that, although poetry is about words, I find the real power sometimes in the things that are not said; those things that clarify themselves internally and remain touched but not completely verbalised. I feel that every word must deserve its space and play its part. Otherwise, writing becomes what our conversations can sometimes be; a way of pushing away real communication. In this sense, verbalisation becomes a barrier to really communicating.

I found this out most profoundly when I attended a short silent retreat. During silence, in the time we spent together as a group, you really understand how verbalising can be a way of putting up a barrier so people do not see your truth. With no words you are stripped back without the usual defences. So for me the secret to the use of words in poetry is to value them and watch that they remain connected and not become just another pushing away.

This book contains a number of poems, some of which contain an obvious thread. As I said before, I don't want to explain every story underneath every poem. I can, however, maybe explain a couple of the stories behind some of them if only to give insight into the experience that underpins my writing.

New Life I wrote at the end of my four-year training in psychotherapy. It was a way for me to thank my trainers and my peers for being there throughout what was a highly emotional and intellectually challenging four years. The Manchester Institute is based on Barlow Moor Road in Chorlton in one of those rambling Edwardian houses. During my time there I entered the building through a big blue front door, which had a coded lock. The main training room was filled with old sofas, tired carpets and woodchip wallpaper. But it became a sanctuary and a place of real challenge for me and I grew from that experience. Out of an original cohort of about twenty, only ten of use made it to the end of the four years. It felt that I had experienced some kind of rebirth and re-nurturing during those years and this fuelled the poem. That experience has only been eclipsed by my recent journey to ordination as an interfaith minister and spiritual counsellor. That is a poem I am yet to write, though.

The Brass Band is my homage to that time in my northern memories when I felt part of something that was part of the very DNA of the community that I was born into. I played in a brass band when I was young and even now the sound of brass awakens emotions in me that remind me of generations of tough and proud people who worked hard and long all week and yet still found time to play rugby and football and light their souls with the sad sound of brass music. Now it seems that the sadness that resonates in this music was carrying a message of the demise of this life. Soon after I left school the restructuring of our economy had begun and the final stage of the demise of that manufacturing age that had sustained those communities came. So a song that grieves those times underpins brass band music.

Little Aaszein is about my mother. Aasein is the root Greek verb from which asthma derives. She was orphaned in the war. Her father had come from a wealthy family and joined the Navy as a rating, marrying a woman his family felt was beneath him. Besides this, her father married, had two children with her mother, a boy and a girl, and then left the Navy to become a window cleaner in Trafford Park. He contracted septicaemia in hospital following a simple hernia operation. These were the days before antibiotics and unfortunately he died. Her mum suffered from asthma and, soon after her husband's death and during the blackout in Manchester one night, she suffered a catastrophic attack. My mum ran the streets trying to find a doctor but by the time they got her mother into a hospital she was already dying. This left two young people without their parents in the middle of a war. My mum remembers not being allowed to attend her mother's funeral and she was taken to see *Sleeping Beauty* instead. But she has a wonderful memory of her father. He had enjoyed a privileged education and so ensured that both his children could write well and have a love of books. So when George V came to open the new Central Library, my mum sat on her father's shoulders to see the King. The first line of this poem is taken from the King's speech that day.

Sonnet to Sonny is a story of my dad's childhood. Once again, as the phony war gathered pace, children were evacuated to the countryside. Twenty thousand children, however, had been fortunate to win a place on the Trans-Atlantic evacuation of children to Canada. Two of these places had been awarded to my dad and his younger sister. So when the other kids went out to the countryside and the schools closed, my dad and his sister were left in the city awaiting their passage. The next ship to make the journey had pulled away from the dockside and my dad and his sister were due to soon make their way to the sea in order to board the next passage.

The *SS City Of Benares* was torpedoed in the Atlantic. Of the ninety or so children on the ship, only thirteen survived. One little boy, Colin Ryder Richardson, was eleven at the time. He was on the *Benares* and, at the dockside when saying goodbye to his mother and father, his mum gave him a bright red jacket that she had made. This was stuffed with flock and was buoyant.

She insisted that he wear this all the time he was on the ship. The jacket probably saved him. Colin actually won a bravery award. At one particular moment he cradled the head of a dying nurse in his arms while they sat in the lifeboat for days struggling to stay awake. All evacuations to Canada were then cancelled. But dad did travel. Not long after this the doctors were concerned about his chest. Asthma again. He was sent to the Welsh coast, to a convalescent home called Dr Garrets. Soon after arriving they found that he had scarlet fever. So he was taken from the home into the countryside of Wales to be isolated with a small group of boys from a local public school. He eventually returned to Dr Garrets, where he made friends with the other children. Some of these were the victims of the bombings in the city. The walked on the beach and talked a lot but they didn't have any proper schooling. Six months later, after not hearing anything from his family during that time, Sonny was placed on the train home. He looked forward to seeing his dad for the first time in six months. But when his dad met him at the station, he just took his case off him and strode ahead of him. No welcome, no hug, and no "great to see you son".

Finally, this summary of some of my poems would not be complete without mentioning *The Kids who Live on the Moon*. I used to live on the moon. Not for a long time. Just for a few brief hours with my friend Paul. Paul was my childhood friend for just a few brief years of my life, between the ages of seven and eleven. We bumped into each other through our teens, but he'd moved house and our relationship had moved on and then we lost touch. He died of cancer when he was in his forties. I don't know where and exactly when. I don't know who he left behind or whether he even remembered me in those last days. It was one of those incidental catch-up conversations when I was up north. I think it might have been my sister who said that phrase, "You'll never guess what? Paul Brereton is dead".

At seven years old I loved the idea of escaping to other worlds. I can recall once spending all morning during my summer holiday in my bedroom wardrobe wishing myself into Narnia. Or staring for hours in a mirror waiting and hoping to see something or someone move on the other side of the glass, or being invited to walk through to that other parallel universe.

Paul did something different. He took what was and wrote us into it, a common practice for kids, but he was a master. So we won the First and Second World Wars, we were the Crusades and the 7th Cavalry at Little Big Horn, and then the week after we were the Mohicans tracking through our imaginary North American forests and transcending the reality of the old slag heaps and derelict garages.

So he taught me how to take the world that was, and create my own agency in that world. Become those people, fight those battles, win those wars, be those heroes. At that time of my life I needed this. I yearned for a friendship that would take me out of my loneliness as the only boy in the family. One that would deepen my understanding of my power to change the way I saw the world. Leave me feeling that I could matter. And I could do great things.

That was what playing with Paul was like. Some thought he verged on madness, but I just thought that he shone in the dark and I always felt part of a great project whenever I was in his presence.

Paul and I were born in 1959. The first ten years of our lives ran parallel with the world's obsession with the space race. Soon after our births, JFK gave the now famous speech in which he declared that the US would have landed a man on the moon by the end of the decade.

I can remember in school and at home how every Saturn V programme was watched with enthusiasm and interest by all ages. As small children, our lives seemed to be preoccupied with the world away from the one we lived on. When I was in my first school we made and played in our own mock-up of a space ship, the space ship that we had imagined and which we had modelled with tin foil and margarine cartons. Television viewing during those years was dominated by each space mission.

So our playtime inevitably relied upon the story of Paul and me – oh, and Richard Forden who was a year younger – blasting into space to visit the moon. We were the generation who were brought up to believe that we could do great things and "walk on the moon" – and we did! The race reached a crescendo in 1969 when the first man actually stood on the moon. I can vividly recall the TV pictures and the flood of photos and images.

But we had been there before them. Yes, Paul and I had blasted off some months before those grown-ups got there, and we lived on the moon! Richard Forden came as well but he had to stay with the mother ship as we steered the landing craft gently onto the Sea of Tranquillity. Actually, Richard had to go home for his tea mid-flight.

It is traditional to acknowledge those who have helped and supported me during my labours towards this book. I thank my best friend John Whitefoot for being my best friend and asking me questions that at times challenged me deeply but from which I have learned so much about myself. I thank Nicole van Zomeren, who helped me to get out there by building my confidence in my work. Clive Johnson, my precious, gentle, spiritual brother who inspires me with his ultimate commitment to his own journey and his belief in me by publishing this work. I thank my friend and fellow "soul groupie" Julia Knowles for the wonderful cover illustration. Then there are my One Spirit brothers and sisters who lovingly held me in their wonderful circle.

This book marks another step in my own journey through my grief for my mum and dad, and of course my dear wife Avril, who all died two years ago. I still feel Avril's presence and know that she is always there in support of whatever I do. I thank her for over thirty years of love, support and fun and for being the mother of my daughter. Our relationship continues in spirit to support me and I give thanks that I had the privilege of being her husband in this life. I thank my daughter Amy, who has blossomed into a young woman who fills me with so much pride, and to Ben, her husband, for occasionally sharing his wife with me. And now I thank my granddaughter, Bobbie, who, although so young, is already teaching me lessons about loving life that I had long forgotten. There are others who have shown their support, love and faith in me over the last few years and I thank them all. They know who they are. Those who, sometimes without even realising it, have been fundamental in me building myself back to a space where life seems whole and magic again.

Now I feel I have said enough. No more explanations, no more stories.

I hope you enjoy these poems. I loved writing them.

A Prayer of Thanks for my Friends

Good friends you have been good to me,
    You pulled together my flesh and bones
        When all I wanted was to follow my love
And have done with this.

Good friends you have been good to me,
    You listened with a kind ear,
        Watched me struggle
And your patience foiled my angry heart.

Good friends you have been good to me,
    Even when I grieved alone,
        You stood guard on my solitary tomb
Awaiting my return.

Good friends you have been good to me,
    I thank you and I know you are good friends,
        For my lover and soul mate taught me
What good friendship is meant to be.

A Painter's Tale

I've had my nose close to the canvas
With sable, ochre, blue and gold,
And I stood back to stretch my body,
Then saw my masterpiece unfold.

It started with a palette of rainbow colours
And a surface pure and white,
I approached and fleshed the background out,
Sometimes working without light.

You have been my beautiful model,
Your pose graceful and so fine,
I've celebrated every inch of you,
Your Dorian image chasing time.

Now I gaze upon this canvass
And I see the faces of my past,
Their eyes look soulfully upon me,
Brushed memories held fast.

I've painted storms way in the background,
And the darker corners of deep red,
The days the tears came as I laboured
Streaming colour trails that bled.

My bones are yearning for their bed now,
My eyes they're closing with their ache,
I place my brushes in cloudy water,
I'll be back when I awake.

It seems a lifetime since that first brush stroke,
When my skin was soft and tight,
Now my lived in callouses and scarring
Betray my toiling through the night.

So when you steal a peek as I slumber,
With my last stroke yet to dry,
Remember my lover you've gazed upon all of me
When we kiss and say goodbye.

A Pebble on the Shore

I feel it there,
    I feel it there, just at the point where
    My stomach meets my breastbone,
Like real love, dead love,
    Lust longing, lost love.

The unfairness of not having
    Knowing someone else has,
Someone else, someone else,
    She gave herself willingly.

She wished them on her,
    Embraced them and let them in,
But then this pebble is smooth,
    Years must pass before
    The tide has worked its magic,
And I have fewer tides than her.

A Prayer of Thanks for my Daughter

Oh my blood
You held me well.

My little girl you accepted your heavy maternal
crown,
Grieving on your coronation.

For the womb that gave you life and pushed you
into this love,
I will be the father I can.

But I am a man.
Please know your mother friend is close now

Sharing in your sadness and your joy,
Accept my gratitude my little girl –
From this little boy.

Brass Bands

The band played
And gently touched my deep fabric,
The cornets holding a beautiful muffled sadness,
Flugel and tenor horns,
Trombones, baritones, euphoniums,
Echoing a shadow fog
Deep in the gut of the basses,
This resonance rises up and whispers our fortune,
Somewhere in our blood
The mucky manuscript containing our demise.

Bodies bent in hot, dangerous, dirty, dark, holes,
Anthracite lungs that felt the pain scare
Of winter frost breathed in,
As they tackled each other to the floor,
Those lungs filled cold tubes with their
Red-faced spittle cough.

Others, deafened by the industry of pure cloth,
Fresh from the smoke
And stale beer smell of billiard rooms
And the musty book lyceum libraries,
Still found that primal pitch
On the nicotine nostrils and moved my soul.

As a young pretender I also played that sad late lament
That pushed those tears up from my gut,
And Whitsun white our tribe marched behind,
On the days when we chased the hell away,
When we celebrated our stubborn humanity.

So play that melancholy masterpiece my salty
comrades,
The one that awakens in me the smell of
Pretty girl soap and sun, and hot tarmac and a promise
not yet broken,
Oh we laughed and kissed and fondled,
And now my youthful heart in memory weeps.

Breakfast Together

She offered me a taste of her omelette,
Suspended on her fork and guided delicately to my
mouth
Like my mouth was her mouth,
She wanted me to share her taste,
Be her senses and melt on her taste buds
I was overcome,
But, as I honour this now,
I remember with sadness
That I didn't reciprocate,
I didn't share my beans.

Butcher's Boy

I was once a Butcher's Boy,
  Too small to slaughter and to cut,
    But old enough to wash in blood
      Of heads and plucks and chicken guts.

I cleaned up after every crime,
  Smell of sawdust, fat and flesh,
    And punched dead pigs in frosted stores
      With face in frozen death mask smile.

Repair the Tear

How do I
Repair the tear?
This delicate cloth,
And every time
I pull with healing thread,
Then the tear it opens up
This delicate cloth,
The scar of my clumsy craft
Too briefly holds,
Then the tear it opens up
This delicate cloth.

I Kick Where I Come From

I kick where I come from,
Despising my false start,
Cringing at past amusements
Undermining flawed foundations,
Shocked at how the years have gone
And I kick where I come from.

I kick where I come from,
Pretend to laugh in fondness
At banal folk tales,
Embellished fantasy features,
The truth is life that's left undone
And I kick where I come from.

I kick where I come from,
The paradox of love and shame,
I embrace then feel deflated,
Knowing this is my blood
From father to son to son to son
And I kick where I come from.

I kick where I come from,
That day that started filled with hope,
Then the diet of dull limits,
Feeling unworthy of my birth right,
Now I see what I've become
And I kick where I come from.

I kick where I come from,
So I need to build a peace
With all this anger in my soul,
Be nourished by the breast of my past,
For soon return when flesh is done
Back to the ground I gaze upon
And I kick where I come from.

Missing

I am the one missing,
   My home is in a missing place,
      I missed the address when I moved in
      And now I see a missing space,
I hear all the voices I missed,
   I reach out and touch the missing me,
      I feel sad I've missed me far too long,
I dream of all these missing pieces,
   I desire the one I miss
      And now I've lost my missing.

Monday Blue

Monday is a colour, blue,
Who smiles on Monday?
Unless the Bank Holiday awards a stay of execution,
The Tuesday becomes Monday,
     Sunday like a lazier Saturday,
And Monday sees how we feel on Sunday.

Usually Sunday gathers momentum,
And we don't want to close our eyes, ending the day,
The evening filled with preparation for the blue,
Shirts pressed,
     Shoes polished too,
Neatly put out for the morning.

Commuting

Tip-tap, tip-tap technology,
   Dog damp overcoats,
Coffee breath through cornflake chins,
   Seven-fifteen, the Triffid trail.

My space, your space,
   Packed in tight three-into-two,
And bedsteads and windows
   Rattle in the wake of the whoosh.

Faces caught in the gravity
   Pulling hearts to the p-way,
Electronic courtesy excuses our bad manners,
   And a smile raises fear and suspicion,
   Don't catch his eye.

Heat

My head goes zing and my ears they pop,
It hits my groin and doesn't stop
And I feel my whole being drop.
And now my heart is blood red raw,
And I don't know what I'm sleeping for
I just want more and more and more.

I'm obsessed with your look, your smell and your touch,
There's nothing that has ever hurt this much,
I'm dangerous but I cannot say,
If you don't feel the same then walk away.

Just to have that love,
To have that beautiful admiration from beauty,
Maybe this pain is meant to be,
I know it hangs on me like an old needy friend,
But to have that love,
To know someone who knows my psalm.

But I won't fight for it, I won't earn it,
I won't pretend it anymore,
No, it must be without effort,
Real love consumes comfortably,
And you dissolve together,
My bones are your bones.

This maybe love I have no doubt,
But just let the sweat and the sex work that one out,
And the thought of that first kiss,
I know people who've killed for less than this.

We dissolve together, we dissolve together,
My bones, your bones, together.
We dissolve together, we dissolve together,
My bones, your bones, together.

I Stand for Something

I stand up.
   That must stand for something,
   So why do I buckle my knees?
I must stand for me,
   Not a gesture
   Otherwise, what are my legs for?

And when I stand
   Don't feel you must sit,
I like to make level contact with your soul
   And what I stand for is for me.

You don't even have to see me stand,
   I can stand alone,
   You won't upset me into my seat,
And I don't stand in opposition,
I must stand for me.

Keep it from the Children

Layered with the jolly armies
Of past muddy traumas,
Pals, mates, muckers,
Feeling all this,
But not seeing,
That's how shame is hidden,
Encrypted beatings,
Giving nothing by letting
That force upon them,
Keeping it from the children
By gifting it to another child,
And then the burden festers
Deep inside a foreigner.

Keep on Breathing

Oh it's such a long time
   Since my history was short,
      And my whole world
         Lived in my pocket.

I owned my space then,
   Then, before they flooded me
      With doubt and fear,
         Then gave me shale mountains to climb.

Keep on breathing,
Keep on breathing my brave child.

Since then, at times
   I have woken at the start, heavy,
      The thought of that first step
         Welding me to the magic mattress.

The very effort of making an effort
   And every part of my being aching to give in,
      But they stand over me and that alone
         Builds an angry energy from my frame,
My marrow kicks in and I climb again.

Keep on breathing,
Keep on breathing my brave child.

On balance have I lived
   A balanced life?
      With all that "tit for tat", "yin and yang"
        And takenawayness.

All that "get back on the horse"
   All that "you've got to laugh"
      All that "things could be worse"
        All that "I'm so sorry to hear".

Penny for your thoughts
   From my lived in pocket,
      Congratulations, you survived,
        Please live and love now my brave child.

Keep on breathing,
Keep on breathing my brave child,
Until it's time to stop.

Leatherette Villanelle

My slippers fit my feet so well,
   I've moulded them through all this time,
So Christmas package go to hell.

With eaten soles that you can tell
   I possess them, they are mine,
My slippers fit my feet so well.

They have such a familiar smell
   That only I could think was fine,
So Christmas package go to hell.

Once upon the stairs I fell,
   Now it's a dangerous decline,
My slippers fit my feet so well.

They have cast a comforting spell
   And I've become what they define,
So Christmas package go to hell.

I'm not going to toll the bell
   On this comforting leatherette sign,
My slippers fit my feet so well,
So Christmas package go to hell.

Up That Ladder

I have no one to foot my ladder,
I climb so fast on lower rungs,
Then I look down and breathe a scare,
I press my body to the frame,
I have no one to foot my ladder,
How did I end up here again?

Life and Love

Life is a fistful of fine sand,
You hold it tight within your hand,
You try to keep it free from harm,
Then revealed an empty palm.

Now all is gone and I'm alone,
A fine sand trail marks the journey home,
And everyone just carries on,
Acting as if you haven't gone.

Whatever happened to the laughter?
The happy happy ever after ?
My colour pallet is all grey,
Now you've left and gone away.

And in my gut a powerless rage,
And in my weeping emptiness I prayed
Then I knew that love had stayed.

Little Aazein

'In the splendid building I am about to open",
    Corinthian Portico, Rotunda Tuscan Colonnade,
I see above the flotsam of the crowd outside
Aazein the Angel, face expectant, excited
    Little breathless bird,
    Perched on those educated
    Shoulders home from sea.

Another night and Aazein cried
As she ran in panic through the blackout streets,
    Fear made a little heart pump
    Hot blood to her temples,
But Snow White had bitten the poisoned apple
    And was laid beside her handsome dead prince,
No life kiss, no happy ever after,
    The fairest of them all was gone,
    And two little bundles just clung on.

Maggie

She sits alone owning her grace,
Her Fenian self destruct button disarmed,
The one that numbed that emptiness left
By those pratie graves when corn was gold,
Her diseased past deceased.

Yet it still colours her landscape,
Filling the horizon in faded greyness,
That was then, when I was there, right back there,
She can still see the smoke trace where she stupored
When she was part of that unbearable sadness.

Now her wide eyed smile placed in the foreground,
Vivid, vital and vibrant
With sweet Maddie love enveloping her whole being,
No longer pulled down into the black earth
  alongside that weeping tribe
And those remains that fed the tumours of her tree.

My Vow

I took a vow,
Like there were several
Lined up neatly on a market stall.

I took a vow,
Was it mine to take?
I didn't buy it.

I didn't barter blindly to get the price down,
I just took it.

I made a vow,
I didn't buy it,
I didn't take it,
I didn't borrow it,
I made it
Out of verbose promising profundity.

Such a big vow
That made me feel small.

I own my vow,
It's not yours, it's mine,
Now I have to keep it,
And watch that I don't break it,
Because if I do then
I will let myself down

Like a forgotten party balloon
Stuck behind the radiator.

New Life

I was born in this room.
Behind the big blue-coded door.
Pushed out onto the tear-stained sofas,
Amongst the woodchip musty paperbacks.
As my head emerged I cried
And something else inside me died.

As I gasped the painful ice of my first breath
My lungs deserted me at times.
Then the calm, calculated call "breathe again",
"And again".

As the light hit my delicate new eyes
Burning salty and warm,
I gazed upon other infants
Wrapped in the swaddling of their survival,
It was then I saw all the love of pink and blue,
And all the love they didn't do.

As my drums defined a listening thud,
I heard your heart
Beat painful hope
And transfuse my warm blood with yours.

As I tasted this bitter sweet milk
At times I despised this breast,
Four long years I suckled and posited,
Sometimes refusing , other times crying in hunger.
It nourished the bones that set me free,
Now I see you and you see me.

So I peek out of the tall window
To where Seamus snoozes,
Under the shade of the bo tree,
Surrounded by eight safe, loved, little girls.

And above them,
Embraced in bo branches,
A small, dark boy with melting smile
And beautiful, excited eyes,
Looks longingly towards the setting sun.
A new adventure has begun.

Nine Twenty-Seven

Blimey, jinkies, lemon squinkies
   Now all is done,
      No more ABC memory
         And counting your wees.

Love stripped back
   So deep,
      Revealing the innocence of
         The atom of "why?"

All those years
   Of ups and downs and ups,
      Punctuated with your love,
         Your clarity of thought.

Always there
   In quiet support,
      Listening, laughing, loving
         And so much presence.

You the musical,
   Every day of your life,
      Your whistle
         And made up songs.

It's a small world after all,
   And we'll drink a drink
      To Lilly the Pink,
         Now everyone's a fruit and nut case.

Thunderbolt of lightning,
   If in doubt leave it out,
      Dah de dah de dah,
         La la la, blah, blah, blah.

Nine twenty-seven, twenty-fourth of June,
   You turn your head
      And whisper one last time,
         "Jim Jar I love you".

I love you too
   My Monkey Moo,
      Thank you,
         Sleep tight, God bless Princess.

The Magpie

There was just one magpie,
    I thought I saw two, but no,
Just one magpie,
    I saluted and wished him good day.

I convince my superstitious self
    That it doesn't make a difference,
Then I see three and my heart races,
    My faith in this silly game returns.

Good morning Mr. Magpie,
    But then I see the second,
And, and I wait for the joy,
    Then someone salutes me.

On Occasion

On occasion, I check in,
   I let the demons loose,
To search my whole being
   For any morsel to feed my script
And on occasion, nothing comes back,
   Then a warm meadow feel.

Like that full on summer day
   Lying back in the dry hay grass,
Eyes closed, no clouds for the season's sounds to echo
   from,
   And a warmth that burns your nostrils.
Eyes closed in this Eden,
   My sex is full and whole.

I can take on the world
   And I soak it in with a deep smile.
Moments like this I crave,
   This is where the light fuels,
Giving you the reason that you search
   Your heart to reference in the darker days.

On the Other Side of the Hill

The climb had been tough,
A steady pace,
Eyes mesmerised at forty-five degrees,
One foot followed another
As my mind and body grabbed the painful gradient.

The breath's meditation
Building to an exhausted crescendo,
When the wobble of my thighs and my airless lungs
Beckoned me to rest
And turn to take the view.

In my sweat-soaked solitude
The panorama revealed its beauty,
A beauty that grew more profound
The closer to my summit,
And memories like jewels seemed
More precious as they became smaller.

Yet further revealed
This wonderful life that I leave behind,
Four points of contact
On the final slippy scramble to my cairn,
The whole fills my dizzy heart,
My tearful soul.

Then I turn to descend the other side of the hill,
But briefly I pause to look ahead at the journey that
greets me.
Now the gravity will work for me,
And all seems in my favour,
Wishing me well, encouraging me to
Embrace the beautiful strange land of greens
And blues and greys.

But I realise that on this side of the hill
I can no longer see the wake of my climb,
And I weep as I strain my memory
For that view once more,
That view of you waving back at me.

Saturday Morning in Grill and Greens

Veneer that mocks and imitates,
   Confusing inside with outside,
The bubbling buzz of empty chat,
   I see I play no part in that.

Excitement of this weekend off,
   And strolling where the weekdays run,
Now lovers sit where we once sat,
   I see I play no part in that.

Sonnet to Little Sonny

Benares boy in buoyant scarlet hug,
He warned my Sonny not to sail the seas,
But little case was packed when chest attacked,
And Doctor Garret kept him safe on shore,
Another scarlet flared and scared his frame,
Then Sonny's case was taken once again,
They travelled unknown mountains to a place
Where isolated posh boys mocked his smile.

With case returned to wounded seagull pals,
They walked and laughed but learning never came,
He dozed and dreamt of lifted hugs from dad,
A full half year alone he clutches case,
But all tears buried in the platform noise,
When dad just snatched his case and strode ahead.

Sonnet to the Blood of Lost Love

My blood is love and so I love my blood,
My love disturbs my blood declares my love,
My blood is hot the passion of my love,
So is my love, so is my blood my love.
I cut my love then runs the blood of love,
The river love that floods my head with blood,
But does your heart survive the blood of love?
So is my love, so is my blood my love.

The pumping round of blood that heats my love,
I could not thrive without that love that blood,
Sometimes I feel our blood is one in love,
And then your blood is cold and spurns my love,
I lose your love and I've no need for blood,
So is my love, so is my blood my love.

That Look

I've noticed everyone's got a look,
　　That look that the mirror cons you with,
　　　　No one shares it,
　　　　　　But everyone has it.
The look usually comes with a walk,
　　Immediate definition.
This is how I want you to remember me,
　　You could have loved this,
　　You don't know what you've missed.

The Bloke who isn't there

You're looking at someone who doesn't care,
I'm the bloke who isn't there,
One day I stopped asking "why?"
And I let the world just pass me by,
I let go of family, friends and living,
And forced them all to stop their giving
By having no more energy to fight,
And making their lovely lives shite
Through my lack of caring or wanting more,
And stopping picking myself up off the floor,
I drink a lot and seldom eat,
And my family avoid me in the street,
I shop at times when others like me
Get treated at the checkouts nervously,
I've just let go and I'm not missed,
I philosophise in the park when I'm pissed,
I frighten children, scare the cat,
I'm told to fuck off and get laughed at,
I've lost every single ounce of pride
When something deep inside me died,
And that's another thing that screws my head,
I'll be like this until I'm dead,
But there'll be no dramatic gesture on the end of a rope,
No penultimate suicide note,

No sudden goodbye and then I'm gone,
I'll just go on and on and on
And on and on till I'm a decrepit old sod,
I'll even outlive that stupid dog
That hung around me all those days,
Two fucking unwanted angry strays,
Then one night I'll bolt up from my chair and die,
Watching repeats of Hi-De-Hi,
And a couple of weeks later someone will complain
There's a nasty smell, it's him again,
Then they'll scrape up what's left of me, shed a
crocodile tear
And disinfect me out of here,
But my demise will put a smile on my neighbour's face,
A nice young couple can buy the place,
Put PVCU windows in and fill it with tat,
Build a lovely conservatory on the back,
So don't pretend sorry and patronise,
I can see your disgust in the back of your eyes,
My skin's so thick, life makes me sick,
And instead of a heart there's a swinging brick,
I'm the one that got away,
Now I just lie in my stinking pit all day
Because you're looking at someone who doesn't care,
I'm the bloke who isn't there.

The Bones of this Man

The bones of this man is the wood of a tree,
  There is no difference in what I see.

The anger of this man is the fear of a mouse,
  There is no difference in what I see
For the bones of this man is the wood of a tree.

The love of this man is the grace of a dove,
  There is no difference in what I see
For the bones of this man is the wood of a tree.

The flesh of this man is the soil of the earth,
  There is no difference in what I see
For the bones of this man is the wood of the tree.

But this man feels guilt, loneliness and shame,
  No other creation feels the same,
The real is dream and dreams are real.

And the bones of this man is the wood of the tree,
  There is no difference in what I see.

Now I See Me

I decided to cross the road
Without your approval,
The road was busy
And I cautioned, looking both ways,
I ignored your considerations,
I ignored that look.

Now I'm disconnected in the park,
That fear gargoyle ate me today,
I want so to run away,
I'm losing all my scaffolding
And I'm expected to stand alone,
Freshly sandblasted, naked again.

The Cobweb Blossom

As I gasp down the Navigation,
The cold morning frost floods my lungs.
That good pain says "I'm still alive",
And the frozen dew exposed a glorious bloom,
All across the flood plane, enchanted by the cobweb
   blossom.

No king ever prized this
Nor gardener nurture it,
Though the engineers who laboured are undone,
Not for our eyes, built to be invisible,
To entrap the ruby-red nourishment.

But for a brief hour all is exposed,
The silent silk spun a beauty
Created by one so feared,
And now I see the gossamer veins
And wrinkles of God's face.

Years ago in the west, in the troubles, khaki bricks of
   young men
Stepped gingerly along similar paths as dawn lifted,
They searched for angel's wings
As, unbroken, they reassured their safe passage,
And at sunset another mundane love letter to say "I'm
   still alive".

The Dressings Came Off Today

The dressings came off my wounds today,
And my doctor told me this, "take it slow",
The wounds of your love were deep
But they have healed as well as they could.

As well as they could?
Look in the mirror, see those scars,
They won't fade much more with time,
A constant external reminder.

Life will carry on,
And there will be many days
When the incident of your tears
Will seem so far away.

But sometimes,
As you awake or sail into slumber
You will feel a deep, dull pain from your old wounds
Reminding you of your unbearable, bearable loss.

I shook his hand,
Said goodbye,
Then exited into the bright
Fresh sunlight of the morning.

I felt the air on my naked scars,
And that dull pain twinge,
But others walked by now
Not noticing my discomfort or the traces of my sadness.

Life goes on and I am here,
I love my beautiful scars, I even love the pain
For it reminds me of how loved I was,
How loved I am and how I can love again.

The Euro Lottery

She won twenty-two million on the Euro Lottery,
But she's keeping her job cleaning the pottery

Down at the offices of Pinkerton-Drew,
It's all around ASDA so it must be true.

She bought a four by four for her husband Bill,
And a Pemberton 8 birth static caravan in Rhyl.

The family are pleased they've broke open the
    beers,
And they've bought their council houses though
    the rent's in arrears.

The bank got in touch two months on,
She's not spent the interest on the money she's
    won.

She could have bought a business down on its luck,
She could have bribed FIFA officials to host the
World Cup.

She could have bought the offices of Pinkerton-
    Drew
And got some other bugger to clean the loo.

Now they eat at the Beefeater every day,
And she's filled her front room with Capo-De-
 Monte.

Her husband Bill and his best mate Ted
Have built a bar in the garden shed.

Now she's chauffeured to work in an expensive
 dress,
A super tax cleaner who shops at M&S.

She's lonely and depressed and that's not funny,
And the money makes money makes money makes
money.

She won twenty-two million on the Euro Lottery,
Now she's given up her job cleaning the pottery.

The Kids Who Live On The Moon

We were the kids who lived on the moon,
From Doghouse to Wendy house to Saturn V,
In Paul's back garden we counted down,
Then Richard Forden left the mother ship,
Returning home for his tea of beef paste butties
And Rowntree's jelly with carnation milk.

For us the war was never cold,
The Hood, THRUSH, The Mysterons,
Always our defeated enemies.
We cherished our freedom,
Always told that the world was ours
Before fear was invented.

We were the kids who lived on the moon,
We took Tizer, chocolate, bread and jam,
We were the kids who lived on the moon,
I'll be going home soon.

Sneaking past mum and dad
With a pocketful of matches and a potato,
Feeling hot exploding excitement,
And wondering why a new excitement
Rose in my blood as I flicked through the
Underwear section of my mum's mail order catalogue.

Our lunar landing was safe and secure,
One large step for a kid,
Then with small steps we kicked the soil,
Played hide and seek, built our den,
Started our fire and pretended to
Devour our raw burnt feast.

We were the kids who lived on the moon,
We took Tizer, chocolate, bread and jam,
We were the kids who lived on the moon,
I'll be going home soon.

Then all was quiet
And we leaned on our beautiful friendship
As we watched the world spin gently by,
And we wondered how long we could stay up here
Before our forced parental rescues,
And the hot sting of the bathwater washed our world
  away.

And then I lay alone between cold sheets
That warmed as I spread out my soft young limbs,
Staring back home through the solitary box room
window.
Today the gravity kids try to hold me down
But I'll be going home soon.

We were the kids who lived on the moon,
We took Tizer, chocolate, bread and jam.
We were the kids who lived on the moon,
I'll be going home soon.

Love Says Goodbye

You sell yourself
   To the highest bidder for your lowest price,
      And there's no change leftover,
         There's more to me than you
And your self-centred scramble to your summit.

There's more to me than you
   And there's more to you than me too,
      You're infatuated with your idea of love
         And real love pecks you on a cold cheek,
It walks by with a tear in its eye.

The New Notebook

When you start writing in a notebook
  You have reluctance,
    You just don't want to spoil
      The nothingness

With your words, scribbles,
  It's as if the marks must be
    Worthy of the taking away
      The nothingness

Now I'm writing,
  Still too many beautiful, perfect, blank pages,
    No chatter, no lies, truth in the white,
      The nothingness

The fresh fizzy smell
  Of unborn new,
    Where it all started,
      The nothingness

Tidy Triolet

With all that happened yesterday,
I've not had time to tidy up,
I find the strength has gone away,
With all that happened yesterday,
So much left for me to say,
But no more coffee in my cup,
With all the happened yesterday,
I've not had time to tidy up.

Tina Christina

Her waters break,
And a precious cargo navigates from her grief-swollen
 womb.
A beautiful boy who secretly fumbles in the dark to
 touch a father's shroud.

Since that time she has also seen others into the world.
And from her small corner of the room she quietly feels
 for all
And counts them out, one by one, as they leave by the
 back door.

Those men, those big strong men
Whose shining shoulders shudder when the waters
 flow,
And now they turn again to her.

And the hands of the clock count down hard lessons
Awakening a little girl's fears,
As her teacher lies cold in the warm sun of his chosen
 shores.

Alone, without the back door key that locks her safely
  in.
Anyone could enter, but no one did,
Nobody saw her in this place

And now they turn again to her,
Those men, those big strong men
Who flinch as they gaze through the watery eyes of a
  fragile little girl

Yet for her an unfulfilled wish,
To see those shining shoulders breathe out and stoop
  down,
To feel the scoop of those enormous hands and smell
  the love of a warm soft embrace

To be lifted up and away from the razor sharp rocks
And the deep, dark tidal pools,
Carried safely home with the warm sun in her face

Those men, those big strong men
Who pretend to protect their own protector,
They missed this little Miss and the little Miss misses
  those water boys.

The End

At the end
We embrace one last time,
Say we'll keep in touch, then touch
But that touch is the last touch,
Turn away and gone
At the end.

A sad phrase, the end,
More sadness than "no",
With "no" you know
There was nothing,
With the end
There was a beginning
And a middle
And a pretend promise of forever.

The end is quiet,
Oh yes, we make noise,
We sing and dance,
We laugh, we cry
As we cruelly reminisce,
Tell jokes of that day,
Or those words.

We kiss, we breathe
For one last time together, but this is near the end,
The end is backs turned
Following that last view,
Our eyes working overtime
Taking snapshots lost for
An album that we browse in those dreams.

No, the end is
The last piece of picked litter,
The last dirty glass washed,
The last payment made,
The last thanks to sad midwives,
The last look across an empty room
As the final echoes of our loud happy sadness fade,
The last door shut, the last deep breath pulling in the
  memory,
Then, the end.

About the Author

Jim Carter is the Tramping Artisan. Born in Oldham, he has enjoyed a successful career in business and currently works as a consultant in a variety of people related areas, including executive coaching, visioning, team working, employee engagement, employee relations and culture change.

He has been fortunate to have worked in a variety of areas during his career. Along the way, he has trained as a tram driver, a prison custody officer and a psychotherapist. He is also ordained as a One Spirit interfaith minister and spiritual counsellor.

In his younger years, Jim was involved in the Manchester music scene. More recently, he has rediscovered his love of poetry and song and now takes every opportunity to sing his songs, tell his stories and recite his poems.

Married to Avril for nearly 29 years, he was widowed in 2013. Jim now lives in Godalming, Surrey.